A SOUND TRACK FOR SIMPLE SOULS

The "A" Side Freestyle

Vol. 1

By

C. K. KADRELL

A Soundtrack for Simple Souls

Vol. 1 The "A" Side

Copyright © 2021 by c. k. Kadrell

CONTENTS

DEDICATION

To the unique and free spirited, to the loud and outspoken, to the perfectly imperfect, to the frequently ignored and completely forgotten, to the angelic and compassionate, to the dreamers and creators, in other words this is dedicated to all the "Simple Souls.".

THE INTRO

To see Life through the eyes of a Simple Soul, is to see Life far beyond Humankind's archaic and petty conflicts, far beyond our imaginary borders, far beyond our social or financial status, far beyond our egos, far beyond our philosophical, religious or political points of view, far beyond our division, far beyond our silence, and far beyond our outright cruelty. In other words, to see Life through the eyes of a Simple Soul is to see Life in its simplest, in its rawest, most beautiful and truest form.

CHAPTER 1:
"THE FALLOUT FROM OUR FLAWS"

Collectively speaking, Human Beings form a truly ingenious species, a point proven by the stunning manner in which we've transformed ourselves from primitive minded cave dwellers into the inventive architects of this industrialized and digitized world we live in today. However, in praising the amazing feats we've achieved as a species, it's impossible to ignore how immensely flawed we are, in fact, our flaws and the subsequent issues that arise from those flaws are the chief reasons why Human Beings haven't evolved to an even higher state of being.

While Human Beings were never meant to be perfect, the problem with our flaws is that we've spent centuries adding further fuel to these flaws by doing little to nothing to address them. We're talking species- endangering flaws such as how deeply divided we are, how supremely selfish we are, how painfully insecure we are, how ridiculously spoiled we are, how perilously arrogant we are, how harshly intolerant we are, how deliberately deceitful we are, how ruthlessly vengeful we are, how shrewdly manipulative we are, how tightly closed- minded we are, how grotesquely greedy we are, how childishly naïve we are, —and as our list of our flaws goes on and on and on.

Although Humanity has been blessed in ways that no other species can claim, in a cruel twist of fate, a large percentage of our flaws is directly related to what is universally viewed as our single greatest strength; our immense and unrivaled intelligence. The chief link between our immense intelligence and our infinite flaws is that Human Beings have become unwitting prisoners of our own superiority complex, a superiority complex born from our belief that we're the most intelligent, the most dominant, the most important species in existence.

When we consider the prominent status in which Human Beings view ourselves it's easy to see how our superiority complex came to be. Yet while it's only natural that Human Beings would see ourselves in such a preeminent manner, the issue with our superiority complex is that not only do we project our feelings of superiority onto all other species of living beings, we also project our feelings of superiority onto our fellow Human Beings. This is an issue which that serves as a major factor behind the coldness and cruelty we display towards one another.

Due to our superiority complex, Humanity Beings have spent centuries dividing ourselves into artificial hierarchies based on trivial differences in our physical appearances, in our belief systems, and in our material possessions. And because of our deep divisions, instead of seeing each other as members of a singular species, we primarily see each other as members of opposing clans, i.e., we see each other as members of opposing genders, as members of opposing races, as members of opposing nations, as members of opposing faiths, as members of opposing social classes, as members of opposing political parties, and any other meaningless manner of division that we can think of.

Another dangerous consequence of our superiority complex is that it causes us to take ourselves far too seriously. And because we take ourselves so seriously, we naturally take our beliefs, our theories, and our personal perspectives far too seriously as well. In fact, we take ourselves so seriously that we feel obligated to attack any beliefs, theories, or perspectives that differ from our own. And it is our feelings of obligation to continuously engage in back-and-forth attacks that keep Humanity stuck in a perpetual state of war with one another.

While it's easy to point fingers at certain nations, certain cultures, certain races, and certain historical figures to serve as examples of how cruel Human Beings can be towards one another, the truth is, there is no nation, is no culture, no race, no social class, no gender, no faith, nor any other category of Human Being that hasn't contributed to our collective coldness and cruelty. And because none of us can claim innocence, we all bare a level of responsibility to do our part to collectively address these issues.

While our superiority complex stands front and center of many of the struggles we face as a species, if we look at our flaws from an individual perspective, the one flaw that sits at the center of most personal struggles is our severe lack of internal understanding. What this means is that there is a large percentage of Human Beings who severely lack an understanding of our inner self, —that oh- so- critical region of our being that houses the very essence of who we truly are.

To understand how our lack of internal understanding is gravely impacting our lives, we need only to compare the amazing things we continue to achieve as a species, with the infinite struggles we face in our personal lives. For instance, while Humanity is collectively adept at pushing ourselves to unimaginable heights, as individuals we're often plagued by prolonged periods of complacency; while as a species we're known for diligently searching for answers to Life's greatest mysteries, as individuals many of us are deathly afraid of any form of in-depth questioning; And while Humankind is collectively renowned for standing tall in the face of adversity, as individuals we have a tendency to surrender to our obstacles and challenges.

Our lack of internal understanding doesn't just inhibit our ability to live up to our individual potential, it also inhibits our ability to see ourselves as unique individuals with our own unique purpose in Life. And it is this inability to see ourselves as unique individuals that makes us highly susceptible to losing ourselves amongst the madness of the masses. What it means to lose ourselves amongst the madness of the masses is that we allow ourselves to be swept up in all of the social chaos and confusion that occurs around us.

Although there is a multitude of factors that contribute to our lack of internal understanding, at the heart of our lack of internal understanding is the external pressures we face in order to live our lives according to the norms and traditions of our social and cultural systems. And the reason we feel this pressure is because the majority of our social and cultural systems have been designed in a manner that promotes mass conformity over individuality and personal freedom. Consequently, due to this pressure what we see are millions if not billions of Human Beings who are living out our daze by shaping our lives around our social and cultural systems rather than shaping our lives around who we are within ourselves.

What we fail to realize about our social and cultural systems is that they do more than define our social and cultural norms, they also play a significant role in shaping how we see ourselves they shape our behaviors, they shape our beliefs, they shape how we see our fellow Human Beings, and they shape how we see the world as a whole. In other words, the majority of everything we perceive, believe, and desire can be traced back to the norms and traditions of the social and cultural systems in which we were raised; consequently, this is also the reason why we often struggle to accept each other when we display beliefs and behaviors that don't align with the norms of our own social systems.

The principal reason our social and cultural systems have maintained such a stranglehold over our lives is because Human Beings have spent countless centuries bullying one another into conformity. In fact, mass conformity is such a critical element of our social and cultural systems that not only are we willing to bully each other into conformity, we're also willing to completely ostracize each other for failing to conform. And it is the fear of being bullied and the fear of being ostracize by our family members, our friends, and by society as a whole whole—that serves as a driving factor as to why we've remained so complicit in our adherence to these antiquated systems.

Although we've been conditioned to believe that bullying each other into conformity is a key component to maintain social and cultural order, we're failing to realize is that by bullying one another into conformity what we're actually forcing each other to live homogenized lives, and our homogenized lives create massive bottle necks where billions of unique individuals find themselves pursuing the exact same things and dreaming the exact same dreams as billions of other Human Beings, —all of which adds further fuel to our already toxic levels of jealousy, greed, insecurity, and self-hatred.

While our lack of internal understanding may seem like a purely personal problem, in reality our internal issues often lead to problems within our interpersonal relationships (both platonic and intimate). And the reason our internal issues often lead to issues within our personal relationships is because our lives are far more intertwined than most of us realize. In fact, our lives are so intertwined that the majority of our actions and decisions have some type of impact on the people in our lives whether the impact is positive or negative.

While our superiority complex, our lack of internal awareness, and the pressures of our social and cultural systems denote some of our most damaging flaws, Humankind's greatest flaw of all is our collective refusal to take an unbiased assessment of ourselves. And what this mean is, that because Human Beings see ourselves as the most dominant species in the universe, and because there are no other living beings capable of showing us the error of our ways, Humanity has essentially spent centuries patting ourselves on our backs while collectively drinking our own Kool-Aid.

A major reason we refuse to address our issues is due to our antiquated belief that our flaws and the subsequent issues that arise from those flaws are the products of Human Nature and the unavoidable consequences of living among billions of Human Beings. However, what we're failing to see and what we've always failed to see is that the vast majority of our issues are not the byproducts of "human nature", or over population; instead, the vast majority of our issues are the byproducts of the archaic ways we look at Life, the archaic ways we look at ourselves, and our archaic adherence to these divisive and shackling systems of living that we've created for ourselves.

While Humankind's hap-hazard refusal to take an honest assessment of ourselves represents a massive roadblock to our ability to effectively address our flaws, the reality we face is that there will eventually come a point in the not-too- distant future when Human Beings will be forced to come together to address our issues, —whether we want to or not. And the reason we'll be forced to come together is because without intervention the present rate of our coldness and cruelty will eventually bring Human Beings to the brink of self-annihilation. Consequently, the longer we remain silent the more pressure we're placing on future generations to shoulder the burden of being forced to save Humankind.

CHAPTER 2:
"LIKE AN INFINITE
BOX OF CHOCOLATES"

While there is a large percentage of people who believe that Human Beings are primarily the products of our environment, a closer examination would reveal that we are primarily the products of our personal perceptions. What this means is that we are the products of how we look at Life; we are the products of how we see ourselves; we are the products of how we see our fellow Human Beings; and we are the products of how we view the world as a whole.

Our personal perceptions do much more than just shape our individual personalities, for it is the diverse nature of our personal perceptions that has helped Humanity to accomplish all the things we've achieved as a species. In fact, the variations in our perceptions are so important to our species that one of the greatest contributions we can make to Humanity is to proactively grant one another the freedom and the space to fully explore and clearly articulate the depths of our unique perceptions.

By granting one another the freedom to fully explore and clearly articulate the depths of our unique perceptions, not only are we promoting peace and tolerance amongst the masses, we're also fostering the formation of a powerful alliance of eclectic souls whose distinctive characteristics will serve as the fuel that keeps Humanity forever traveling in the direction of constant progression.

Ultimately, our thoughts, our emotions, our beliefs, and our personal perspectives all combine to form our unique personalities. Our unique personalities essentially serve as the soundtrack to our souls, and each and every Human Being was born with an inalienable right to not only sing our own unique songs, but to sing our unique songs as loudly and as passionately as we choose.

Instead of allowing ourselves to become distracted by the tone in which a message is delivered or by the appearance of the message deliverer, our principal objective and responsibility should always be to determine if there is any degree of discernable truth in the message --regardless of the tone or the appearance of the person delivering the message.

Is it possible that this thing we call Life is so much more than Human Beings have long perceived it to be? Is it possible that the universe is infinitely larger than what our scientific theories have led us to believe? Is it possible that the entity we call God or Allah or The Grand Creator is far different from what Human Beings have long perceived he, she, or it to be? And if all these "ifs" are indeed true, could it also mean that Human Beings are so much more than what we've long perceived ourselves to be?

Humankind's willingness to critically examine ourselves from an individual and collective perspective will significantly increase our ability to identify and subsequently understand the real reasons why we look at Life the way we do, why we do the things we do, why we feel the way we feel, why we strive for the things we strive for, and so forth.

Human Beings struggle to see Life from a big picture perspective, not only are we fail to fully appreciate how blessed we are to be alive, we also fail to appreciate the natural beauty, the simplicity, the unpredictability, and the sheer immensity of Life. And ultimately our blindness prevents us from recognizing that above all other things, it is Life that reigns supreme --for it is Life that allows Human Beings to do all the things that we do as Human Beings.

If we took the time to look at the world around us while completely ignoring all the things that have been invented by Human Beings (the roads, the buildings, the houses, the cars, the clothes, the gadgets, our social and cultural norms and traditions etc. etc.), the only things we would see is would be the natural landscape of our planet and, the various plants and animals that share the planet with us— and then we would see ourselves, meaning we would see billions of butt- naked Human Beings scattered all across the planet. And this hypothetical view of Life beyond Humankind's inventions is actually what Life really is and what it has always been.

Hypothetically speaking, what if Human Beings are "naturally good," yet we turn to deceit and cruelty and other self-serving behaviors only after we've allowed ourselves to believe that being good is the least effective means of satisfying our own selfish needs? And if this hypothetical theory is indeed true, should it not inspire us to reassess the nature of our "needs," especially if our so called "needs" have the ability to completely override our natural state of being?

C. K. Kadrell

Although Angels typically come to us in our dreams or in fleeting visions, there are rare occasions when Angels appear before us in Real Life. And when Angels appear before us in Real Life, not only do they bless us with their presence, they also bless us with their compassion, with their guidance, and with their unconditional Love. With that said, it's our responsibility as Human Beings to recognize these Real-Life Angels when we encounter them.

R.I.P to My Mother 1952—-2021

Too often we speak to one another just to shoot the breeze. Seldom do we speak to one another for the purpose of arriving at a mutual understanding; seldom do we speak to one another for the purpose of strengthening our strained relationships; seldom do we speak to one another to express how we truly feel; seldom do we speak to one another to exchange new ideas or to share our deepest desires or even our deepest fears. In other words, seldom do we speak to one another for the purpose of addressing the things that truly matter.

Although we often talk about such things as brotherly love or loving thy neighbor or how we're searching for our one true love, the reality is that the more divided we become the harder it is for us to love one another. The reason is because it's difficult to love someone that we've been conditioned to hate; it's difficult to love someone we don't fully understand; it's difficult to love someone we don't fully trust; it's difficult to love someone we're secretly competing against; it's difficult to love someone who possesses something that we feel we deserve; it's difficult to love someone who has beliefs and perspectives that differ from our own... In other words, it's difficult to love someone, anyone, when most of the things we do as Human Beings have little or no relation to fostering Real Love.

There is a large number of Human Beings who subscribe to the mythology that the more physically attractive we are or the higher we stand on social and economic ladders, the more insulated we become from feeling any degree of pain or disappointment. Yet, for those of us who live in the real world, we share in the understanding that a person's physical appearance, regardless social status, person's age, person's gender, person's race, and regardless of any characteristic we can name, no single Human Being will ever be exempt from experiencing the same pains and disappointments that are inevitably experienced by all Human Beings.

For those of us arrogant enough to believe that we are in fact immune to heartache or pain, when we inevitably encounter moments of heartache or pain our most common response is to immediately fall to our knees pleading towards the sky screaming, "Why me, why me?" "Why am I being punished?" "Why is the world so cruel to me?" "Why me, why me?" But again, for those of us who live in the real world, our most common response is, "W why not me?"

Strangely, some of our most common methods of problem resolution are also our most ineffective methods of problem resolution. And some of these ineffective methods include how; we completely ignore our issues: we passively hope and pray that our problems will just magically go away; we pour ourselves into a series of distracting activities, or we rely on others to provide us with solutions to our personal problems. The reason such methods are ineffective is because without our own direct intervention the majority of our personal problems will continue to resurface —in fact, they're likely to get even worse.

When it comes to examining our present daze, we should begin by asking ourselves a few fundamental questions. The first question we must ask is: How is it possible that we can wake up each morning without realizing it's a brand- new day? The second question is: How is it possible that we can spend hours upon hours in front of our mirrors while never truly examining ourselves? And the third question is: How is it possible that we spend the majority of our "daze" attempting to consume everything within our sight, yet we seldom make any concerted effort to feed our souls?

Human Beings have a tremendous fear of that which we don't understand, and for many of us, our greatest fear is the fear of being alone with ourselves. And our fear of being alone with ourselves serves as one of the main reasons that Human Beings tend to run in frightened packs. It's also the reason why we accept subpar treatment from the people in our lives, —as we're willing to tolerate any kind of treatment as long as it keeps us from having to deal with the frightening emptiness that we feel within ourselves.

To understand the difference between a sheep and an eagle is to understand that there are some people who possess a clear understanding of their worth, a clear understanding of their individual purpose, and a clear understanding of the infinite pitfalls associated with the social and cultural games we force each other to play. While on the other hand, there are those amongst us who understand none of these things.

While we often go out of our way to avoid any type of conflict, the truth is, not only is conflict inevitable, there are times when conflict is absolutely necessary, — especially when we experience conflicts within ourselves. The reason that it's necessary to have internal conflicts is because our internal conflicts signify that there are certain aspects of our beliefs and perceptions that pose both an immediate and a long- term threat to our inner peace and our continued growth.

Learning how to protect our energy from people who have a propensity of draining our energy is a critical life skill. And what it means to protect our energy is to know within ourselves that it's perfectly okay to say, "Not today.", It's perfectly okay to say, "Not this week.", It's perfectly okay to say, "Not this month.", Iin fact, it's perfectly okay to stretch this period of "not okay" to any length of time we choose. And the reason all of these periods of separation are perfectly okay is because when it comes to protecting our energy, it's our responsibility to do so do by any means necessary.

We live in a strange age where every minute of every day we're forced to look over our shoulders in order to protect ourselves from a myriad of hidden dangers. And sadly, the majority of these hidden dangers are posed by our fellow Human Beings. And while we shouldn't have to live in fear of one another, the reality is if we fail to acknowledge the greed and cruelty that exists amongst Human Beings, then we're only increasing our odds of eventually falling victim to one of the many predatory Human Beings who sustain themselves by fiendishly feasting upon those who are either exceedingly naïve or noticeably vulnerable.

Due to the extreme coldness and cruelty that Human Beings display towards one another, there are some who believe that we're actually living in Hell, and we just don't realize it. However, when we consider how blessed we are to be alive and how blessed we've been as a species, there's reason to believe we're actually living in Heaven, and we just don't realize it. And the reason we fail to realize this is because we're being subconsciously bombarded and misguided by our own internal issues, —issues that we ironically label as our personal demons.

Although we often make the saintly claim that "we couldn't hurt a fly", such assertions are categorically untrue; and the reason such assertions are categorically untrue is because not only is each of us responsible for killing our fair share of defenseless flies, whether intentional or not, each of us is also responsible for inflicting our fair share of heartache and pain upon the people in our lives.

C. K. Kadrell

The most effective way to significantly reduce the amount of frustration and disappointment we feel towards our family members and close friends (as well as perfect strangers) is via the understanding that regardless of what we expect from one another, the reality is that we're all just ordinary people, and at the end of the day, people can only be people.

Isn't it strange how it's perfectly acceptable to openly express pride in our clothes, in our cars, in our homes, in our cities, in our schools, and even our favorite sports teams, yet we're made to feel guilty for expressing the same level of pride in just being our natural selves? Then again, maybe displaying pride in just being our natural selves isn't the real issue, —maybe the real reason we perceive this as being so wrong is due to the infrequency in which we see each other expressing pride in our natural selves.

As Human Beings we often spend our daze chasing after one thing or another, and one of the chief reasons we spend our daze chasing after endless things, is due to our desperate desire to be perceived as "something,", and by something, it means something worthy of attention, something worthy of respect, something worthy of praise, something worthy of love. Yet, what many of us fail to realize is that from the moment we were born into the world we were already deemed worthy of all of these things.

Despite the infinite ways in which Human Beings attempt to divide and define ourselves, when we look at ourselves from a core perspective, meaning when we look at ourselves based on the core of who we are as Human Beings, the truth is no matter our social status, our race, or our nation, in the grand scheme of all things every Human Being falls into one of four distinct categories: The Oppressors, The Oppressed, The Indifferent, and The Defiant. And the category that we fall into has a profound impact on how we see ourselves and how we see and treat our fellow Human Beings.

C. K. Kadrell

While there is a multitude of factors that helped propel Humankind into the position of dominance that we hold today, one of the most important of these factors has been our ability to freely explore every inch of our planet in search of lands that provided us with better opportunities to enjoy more fruitful, more fulfilling, and more sustainable lives. A fact which that is rather ironic considering how in our present daze we limit each other's opportunity to experience a more fulfilling Life by enforcing imaginary laws at imaginary borders.

In order to acknowledge the immense contributions that were made by mankind's ancient ancestors, we must start with the understanding that regardless of how expansive or how small a particular culture or civilization grew to be, regardless of the length of time that a certain civilization or culture remained in existence, in the grand scheme of all things, every single civilization and every single culture that has ever existed played their own uniquely important role in contributing to the advancement of Humanity.

If we were to measure the evolution of our species in the same manner that we measure the life span of an individual person, i.e., from new born, to infancy, to toddler, to child, to preteen, to teen, to adulthood, to middle age, to senior citizen—based on how childish, how naïve, how spoiled, and how selfish we are as a species, it's safe to say that we Human Beings are still in our "preteen" phase.

In a perfect world, an individual's right to freely exist as they choose to exist should always hold precedent over any form of forced adherence to any of Humankind's assorted beliefs, theories, or perspectives. Yet as we all know, these strange and restrictive systems of living that Human Beings have created for ourselves are anything but perfect.

When it comes to choosing a side in this universal war against individuality and personal freedom, there is no such thing as a taking a neutral stance; as we are either passionate advocates of individual liberty or at the very least, passive advocates of selective oppression.

At some point in each of our lives we inevitably arrive at a Life- defining cross roads. And it is at this crossroads we must choose between spending the rest of our lives following the beaten path of the masses, or follow a path that is aligned with our own unique and independent spirits. The key to making a well- formed decision at these moments is to ensure we have a firm understanding.

Within each and every one of us resides a powerful and inspiring voice, and the primary purpose of this voice is to guide us towards a personalized path of happiness and individual freedom. Yet, the problem we're facing is that only a small percentage of Human Beings possess the ability to hear our internal voices, and the reason we struggle to hear our internal voices is because we've been conditioned to ignore our inner voices while silently obeying the hollow voices of the masses.

Humankind's widespread practice of just copying and pasting memes on social media is merely a replication of the copy and pasted manner in which Human Beings approach our real life social and cultural systems. And what this means is that for most of us we've adopted the philosophy that it's far safer and far more convenient to just mimic other people's thoughts, other people's beliefs, and other people's actions instead of being and expressing our own authentic selves.

It's funny how Human Beings are so leery of cults yet we fail to acknowledge or denounce our own involvement in them. What this means is that the moment we're born into the world it marks the beginning of our indoctrination into our particular social and cultural system of existence. And the reason we fail to acknowledge or denounce our own involvement in a cult is because we mistakenly see our social and cultural norms and traditions as the core of our human existence, —when in reality these are just habits and beliefs and games that we've invented to keep ourselves entertained while we try to figure out this grand phenomenon called Life.

The reason so few us are willing to question or challenge the norms and traditions of our social and cultural systems is because the idea of challenging these systems seems like a blatant act of blasphemy, and the reason we feel this way is because we typically learn our social and cultural norms from our parents, grandparents, great grandparents, and other elders whom we hold in high regard. Yet the problem with this rationale is that much like ourselves, our elders should have also challenged our social and cultural systems.

While it's obvious that Human Beings need some form of law and order to keep us from slipping into a state of total chaos, what we don't need and what we can no longer afford to do, is to continue believing that our social systems represent the definitive means by which all Human Beings are meant to exist. In fact, it is Humankind's blind loyalty to these archaic social systems that serves as one of the primary things that keepings Human Beings from overcoming many of the issues that have plagued us for centuries.

While there are certain phrases that are typically dismissed as just meaningless clichés, there are also certain sayings that are undeniably true, take for instance the old adage that "of all the people we hurt, it's the people we love who we tend to hurt the most." And to prove how true this saying is, —if we were to catalogue all the pain, all the sorrow, all the greed, all the selfishness, all the deception, all the betrayal, all the regret, and every other form of emotional turmoil present in the world, --we would discover that a large percentage of these injurious actions is directly related to the strained relationships we have with our family members and close friends.

C. K. Kadrell

What if Human Beings have spent centuries looking at a Love from a completely flawed perspective? Meaning, what if Love isn't about possession or ownership or appearances or even appeasing our own desires? What if Love (meaning, Real Love) is about simply loving another Human Being and truly wishing to see them live as happily and as freely as they possibly can?

The people who truly love us don't care if we're of a socially acceptable size; they don't care if we drive a particular type of car; they don't care what kind of clothes we wear; in fact, the people who truly love us don't care about any of those superficial traits. Instead, the people who truly love us well they love us because they see us and appreciate us for who we truly are.

A large percentage of our intimate relationships consist of one person whose thoughts and actions are primarily based on the betterment of the union; while on the other hand, the thoughts and actions of their partner are primarily based on the betterment of his or herself. And in such relationships, while one partner looks at the relationship from an "us" perspective and the other from a "Meme" perceptive, it is typically the partner with "The Me" perspective who consistently finds a way to paint themselves as the victim during conflicts and disagreements.

While our intimate relationships are naturally challenging, they become far more challenging when we mistakenly allow ourselves to believe that these intimate relationships are nothing more than a contemptuous tug of war— a war we engage in for the sole purpose of determining which of us shall be crowned the undisputed ruler over a disingenuous union.

The reasons that so many Human Beings struggle to find our one True Love is because it's extremely difficult to find our one True Love when we've yet to find ourselves. In fact, even if we were lucky enough to find our one True Love before discovering ourselves, it's highly unlikely that we were be able to recognize this person for who they truly are and the role they're meant to play in our lives.

Far too often we bottle up our dreams, simply because they seem impossible to achieve. Yet, what we fail to realize is that the reason we believe our dreams are impossible to achieve is because we spend our daze inventing a litany of possible obstacles that could prevent us from achieving our dreams. And what this ultimately means is that the more we focus on things that might prevent us from achieving our dreams, the more we allow our dreams to sink deeper and deeper into a self-defeating sea of self-doubt.

While there is a proven correlation between work ethic and personal achievement, there's a vast number of people who seek the rewards of success while refusing to put in any of the prerequisite effort needed to achieve it. And the reason we fail to put in the prerequisite effort needed to achieve our goals is because deep down we're afraid to fail, and the primary reason we're afraid to fail is because we don't want to be perceived as a failure in the eyes of others.

When it comes to pursuing our dreams, it is never enough to have a single plan; instead, we must have backup plans and back up plans for our backup plans. This way, even if our primary path to achieving our dreams begins to rapidly unravel, instead of panicking or giving up on our dreams, our backup plans allow us to remain stoically composed— as we have already established an elaborate network of alternate routes.

C. K. Kadrell

While human nature compels us to complain when our plans are disrupted by a sudden downpour of rain, these unforeseen storms serve as symbolic reminders of the unpredictability of Life itself; for rarely, if ever, do the events in our lives perfectly coincide with our pompous expectations of continual sunshine.

Although we often view change with fear and disdain, what frequently goes unnoticed and unappreciated is the crucial role that change plays in fueling our maturity. And because of the crucial role that change plays in our continued growth, as both a species and as an individual person, whenever we find ourselves faced with change, instead of fighting against it we should fully embrace it, as it is likely to serve as a catalyst in the next phase of our collective and personal development.

Through maturity and faith, we learn to accept and embrace the fact that there are certain events that occur in our lives that were meant to occur; there are certain emotions we were meant to feel; there are certain challenges and certain obstacles we were meant to face; there are certain thoughts we were meant to think; and there are certain challenging decisions that we make that we were meant (destined) to make.

What we gain from engaging in a love affair with Life, is an intimate understanding that no matter how troublesome our situations or circumstances seem to be, the fact that we're still breathing, still feeling, and still thinking, serves as a powerful reminder that despite our challenges we still have endless reasons to rejoice. In other words, there is no set of circumstances or problems that is large enough to overshadow the fact that we're still blessed to be alive.

While we have undoubtedly achieved a lot as a species, still we must be careful to never allow ourselves to believe that Human Beings are the fuel that makes the world go around. The reason we must never allow ourselves to believe such a foolish thing is because although we are the most dominant species on the planet, the reality is that our entire species could easily be gone tomorrow, and even in our absence this colossal planet that we call Earth would continue spinning upon its axis.

Despite Humankind's immense intelligence, possessing the ability to definitely decipher the true meaning of "Life" is a task that far exceeds the mental capacity of even the most brilliant Human Beings. Consequently, when we encounter Human Beings who professes to possess such knowledge and skill, no matter how divine their words may sound, their statements should be viewed as nothing more than personal declarations of pure speculation.

Although we tend to view Life from a human perspective, the truth is, Life in its most universal sense encompasses not only human existence but every single thing in existence. And what this means is that Life in its truest sense encompasses the existence of the most distant planets, the most distant stars, and the most distant moons—all the way down to the smallest grains of sand on Earth. And it is the extraordinarily complex interplay between the universes various entities, energies, and still unanswered mysteries that combine to represent Life in its truest most universal sense.

A perfect example of Humankind's extreme arrogance is the fact that during our 50-plus years of space exploration we've only explored about four percent of the known or "visible" universe; thus, the remaining 96 percent of the known or "visible" universe remains a complete mystery. With that being said, despite our extremely limited view and understanding of the immensity of the universe both "visible" and still unseen, the average Human Being still finds it impossible to believe there could be other forms of intelligent life in the universe other than Human Beings.

Despite our countless theories about the creation and overall makeup of the universe, there are aspects of the universe that are likely to forever remain mysteries to Human Beings. Take for instance our widely accepted notion that the universe was birthed by the "big bang." And while the big bang is certainly a sound theory, at least based on the data presently available to Human Beings. What we've yet to determine is from what source did the various elements that combined to form the big bang originate from, and from what source did that original source originate from— and to add to that, is it possible that the present iteration of the universe is merely a product of a series of previous big bangs?

If God has a human- type ego, as Human Beings tend to believe, then instead of taking pleasure in being robotically worshipped as a supreme being, wouldn't a supreme being be far more impressed by our Human Beings' collective ability to fully acknowledge and truly appreciate everything that (it, he, or she) has brought into being? Which happens to include fully acknowledging and truly appreciating our individual lives as well as the lives of our fellow Human Beings?

Many of the things that Human Beings label as blessings are merely the shallow by-products of our naïve obsession with material possessions and social acceptance. And because we suffer from such a distorted view of what a blessing really is, we fail to realize just how naturally blessed we truly are. And what it means to be naturally blessed is that we are blessed to be alive; we are blessed in our ability to experience the world around us; and we are blessed in our ability to share our life experiences with our family and friends.

If our goal is internal growth, then we cannot avoid the critical act of self-evaluation; instead, we must daringly dive into the deepest depths of ourselves and carefully examine who we truly are. For we can neither understand nor improve any aspect of ourselves that we are too bored, too frightened of, or too embarrassed to acknowledge.

Regardless of whether we consider ourselves to be religious or not, every Human Being should understand how blessed we are to be alive. But unfortunately, many of us are failing to realize this fact, and the reason we fail to understand how blessed we are to be alive and the overall value of our lives, is because Human Beings have become completely tone deaf to the things that truly matter in Life.

A word of warning to those whose lives are ruled by the pursuit of monetary riches. This warning is that while money is an undeniably vital part of our lives, we must be careful that we don't ignore the lavish and lasting rewards of finding prosperity within our natural selves—for when our financial fortunes collapse into total ruin, as they so often do, it is the immense richness of our souls that shall fortify us with an enriching reminder of our true value.

C. K. Kadrell

While it's extremely difficult for Human Beings to see the flaws of our belief systems, the truth is, any system of belief (or philosophical point of view) whose foundation is based on the elevation of one group of Human Beings above all other Human Beings should be universally viewed for what it clearly is; a hateful, agenda driven doctrine born from the darkened hearts and minds of truly broken souls.

Although it may be difficult to admit, the reality is that the majority of the problems we encounter in our personal lives are not the result of enemy sabotage or some unavoidable consequences of living in a cold and unjust world. Instead, the majority of the problems we encounter in our personal lives are a direct result of our own ill-fated decisions. And until Human Beings start taking personal responsibility for our ill-fated decisions, we will never be able to overcome our self-inflicted miseries.

The reason modern Human Beings often fail to learn from the mistakes of our ancient ancestors is because far too many of us view history as some mythical period of time that has little relevance to our present-day lives; yet if we were to look at history, as history is meant to be viewed, we would realize that history serves as the origin story of our present daze.

Isn't it strange how Human Beings invest so much of precious time and energy bickering back and forth over our conflicting interpretations of the ancient past, yet at the same time we're investing little time or energy towards addressing the blatantly obvious challenges that we face in our present- day lives?

While it's difficult for Human Beings to manage our natural arrogance, the problem we run into. when we see ourselves standing at the center of the world is that not only do, we create unrealistic expectations and place unnecessary pressures on ourselves, our arrogance also leads us to view our obstacles and challenges as being much larger than they really are.

CHAPTER 3:
"THE NEW DAY CO-POP"

Although we typically speak of Indigenous people in reference to the people who occupied a particular land during a particular period in time—from a big picture perspective—Humanity as a whole represents the Indigenous people of Earth, and subsequently as the Indigenous people of Earth, we jointly represent one people, one tribe, one culture, and one nation.

There are endless reasons why Human Beings see ourselves the way we do; there are endless reasons why we treat each other the way we do; and there are endless reasons why we see the world and Life as a whole the way we do. Ultimately, it's our collective responsibility as Human Beings to invest the time and energy required to identify the root causes of these endless reasons— as it is only then, can we effectively address our endless issues.

Scattered all across the globe are millions of weary souls, all of whom have grown tired of trying to single- handedly shoulder the burdensome weight of an entire world, —or to be more specific, there are millions of scattered and isolated souls who are single-handedly trying to save the whole of Humanity. Which begs the question of why? Why should only millions of Human Beings bear the responsibility of saving the whole of Humanity when there are nearly eight billion Human Beings in the world?

Although it's easy to say that we're here to lend our support to one another, the reality is that more often than not, instead of lending our support to one another, we quietly stand on the sidelines and watch each other struggle. All of which begs an important question, and that question is this; If we aren't sharing with one another, if we aren't respecting one another, if we aren't protecting one another, if we aren't learning from one another, if we aren't inspiring each other if we're not uplifting one another, if we're not empowering each other, then what exactly are we doing for one another?

When we find ourselves in the midst of a brand-new day, not only are we presented with new opportunities to experience Life in brand new ways, we're also presented with new opportunities to learn from yesterday's mistakes. Yet, our ability to take full advantage of the new opportunities presented by our brand-new days is largely dependent on our ability to understand that every day is indeed a brand- new day.

Regardless of the species, every new generation of living being bares an innate responsibility to not only carry on the legacy of their predecessors, but more importantly, bare a responsibility to improve upon the shortcomings of their predecessors. And the reason every generation bares this responsibility is because every generation is responsible for creating a brighter future for the generations that will eventually follow them.

For those of us who are consumed by a sense of personal responsibility to do our part to help enlighten and inspire our brethren, it's imperative that we also understand that regardless of how much we desire to see our fellow Human Beings rise to new heights, at the end of the day, none of us possess the ability to show someone something their mind is ill-prepared to see—even when what's shown to them is a vision of their own unique and immense capabilities.

More often than not, the people who we label as heroes, saints, and saviors are none of these things; they are simply ordinary people who felt compelled to do more than just sit around and passively observe another's misfortune. In fact, one could argue that our use of such valiant labels such as heroes, saints, and saviors is a clear indication of the appalling degree of apathy that has fallen upon Humanity.

One of the best things we can do as parents, as guardians, and as adults in general, is to teach our children about the critical importance of acknowledging, understanding, and fully embracing their inner selves. And the reason it's so critically important that we teach our children to embrace their inner selves is because doing so will create a dramatic change in how our children see themselves and how they deal with the world around them. But in order for us to teach our children this critical life skill, we as adults must begin by teaching it to ourselves.

When it comes to measuring our value as Human Beings, contrary to what we've been led to believe, there are no true hierarchies amongst Human Beings. In fact, the only things that truly separates one Human Being from another, are the subtle and not so subtle differences between our individual perspectives and the manner in which we deal with our individual circumstances. Anything beyond that is strictly a material matter (a matter of material possessions that is), and in the grand scheme of things our material possessions have absolutely nothing to do with our value as Human Beings.

C. K. Kadrell

If Human Beings are to ever see one another in our truest and most natural form, then we must collectively put an end to our archaic practice of classifying and judging each other according to the color of our skin—as this is the only way that Human Beings will ever free ourselves from these race- based cages that have collectively enslaved us for countless centuries.

When it comes to the random circumstances that each of us was born into, the reality is this: not a single Human Being had a choice in determining who our parents and extended family would be; not a single Human Being had a choice in determining what our race or gender would be; not a single Human Being had a choice to what country of origin or what belief system we would be born into; not a single Human Being had a choice in determining what social-economic conditions we would be born into. But there is one choice that has been afforded to every Human Being, and that choice is our ability to determine the type of person we become, the type of Life we live, and how the way we treat our fellow Human Beings.

Whether we realize it or not, Human Beings are meant to learn and grow from our mistakes instead of just rolling over and wallowing in self-pity—consequently each of us has a personal responsibility to turn our mistakes, as well as our obstacles and challenges, into enriching stepping stones.

Of all the things Humanity needs to do to strengthen and improve our species, more than anything, we need more Human Beings who truly know themselves, more Human Beings who believe in themselves, more Human Beings who are capable of thinking for themselves, and more Human Beings who are capable of effectively navigating Humankind's endless pitfalls. Yet in order to facilitate these things, above all else, what Human Beings truly need is more Human Beings who willingly accept the challenge of sharing their understandings with their fellow Human Beings.

C. K. Kadrell

While it's certainly a challenge to see ourselves as unique individuals with our own distinct purpose in Life, there is one fundamental truth that every Human Being should firmly understand—and that fundamental truth is this, although we may look similar, speak the same languages, share the same spaces, and share similar life experiences, there is no denying that every Human Being represents a unique being with a unique existence and unique purpose in Life.

Once Human Beings start placing an equal amount of value on our internal selves as we place on our social selves, we'll start to look at Life completely differently, —we'll start to looking at ourselves completely differently; we'll start to looking at the people around us completely differently; we'll start look at our so-called issues and problems completely differently; and we'll even start looking at our so- called needs and desires completely differently.

Imagine how vastly different the world would be if Human Beings made a commitment to give back to world the same things that we take from the world; for example, if we desire happiness and love, conversely, we'd also feel a sense of personal responsibility to infuse happiness and love back into the world. If we desire wealth and prosperity, we would also feel a personal responsibility to help the people around us also achieve some level of wealth and prosperity, and if we desire freedom and equality, we would also feel a personal responsibility to do our part to help promote freedom and equality for all of Humanity.

Embarking on a journey of self-discovery is about so much more than enhancing our understanding of our individual selves—a journey of self-discovery is also about enhancing our understanding of the people around us as well. And what this means is, despite our perceived differences, at our core, Human Beings are all the same, —meaning we have the same basic emotions, the same basic desires, the same basic needs, and the same basic fears. And because of these facts, the more we learn and understand about our individual selves, the more we learn and understand about Humanity as a whole.

In the same way that a journey of self-discovery entails far more than just enhancing our understanding of our individual selves, coming together to collectively address our long-standing issues entails far more than just improving the lives of modern-day Humans. In fact, more than anything, collectively addressing our long- standing issues is about creating a more fruitful foundation for the generations of Human Beings who will eventually follow in our footsteps.

Although we have been led to believe that it's impossible for a single individual, or even a small group of people, to make any kind of significant difference in the world, what we must understand is this. When fueled by unyielding faith, patience, and perseverance, even a seemingly insignificant spark possesses the potential to blossom into a breathtaking flame.

Our ability to continue rising as a species largely hinges on our collective willingness to look far beyond our imaginary differences. And the reason this is true is because once we learn to look beyond our imaginary differences, we'll finally realize just how infinitely connected we really are. And once we finally acknowledge how infinitely connected, we are, we'll be a point where we can begin to completely redefine what it means to be a Human Being.

It's rather telling that among the numerous holidays celebrated by Human Beings, there isn't a universally celebrated holiday dedicated to just being a Human Being. A day in which Human Beings put aside our petty differences by coming together to collectively celebrate all that we've achieved as a species.

THE SIMPLE SOUL COLLECTION

A Soundtrack for Simple Souls Vol. 1
The "A" Side (Book)

A Soundtrack for Simple Souls Vol. 2
The "B" Side (Book)

Questions For Your Reflection (Book)

Warm Words for a Cold World
(Audio Download)